MOODS OF SUSSEX

A PORTRAIT OF A MUCH LOVED COUNTY

IAIN McGOWAN

HALSGROVE

First published in Great Britain in 2006

Title page photograph: *The view from the slopes of
Ditchling Beacon looking inland across the Sussex Weald*

British Library Cataloguing-in-Publication Data
A CIP record for this title is available from the British Library

ISBN 1 84114 529 7
ISBN 978 1 84114 529 7

HALSGROVE
Halsgrove House
Lower Moor Way
Tiverton, Devon EX16 6SS
Tel: 01884 243242
Fax: 01884 243325
email: sales@halsgrove.com
website: www.halsgrove.com

Printed and bound by D'Auria Industrie Grafiche Spa, Italy

CONTENTS

Milestone at Wych Cross, Ashdown Forest. As turnpike trusts were formed in the late eighteenth and early nineteenth centuries, milestones were erected alongside the improved roads. The succession of these posts along what is now the A22 from East Grinstead over Ashdown Forest and down towards the coast is one of the longest in the country. Note the bow of ribbon and bell design alluding to Bow Bells in the City of London from where the mileage was originally measured.

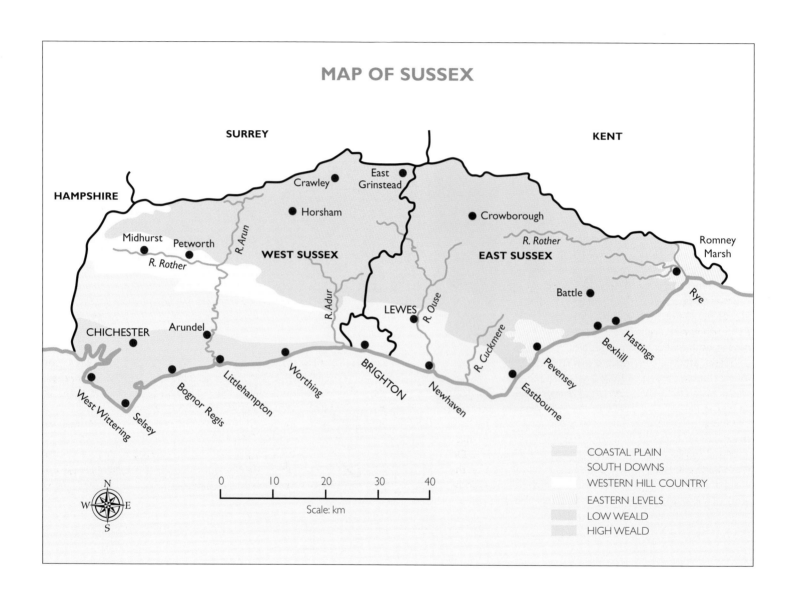

MAP OF SUSSEX

SURREY

KENT

HAMPSHIRE

Crawley

East Grinstead

Horsham

Crowborough

Midhurst Petworth

R. Arun

WEST SUSSEX

R. Rother

Romney Marsh

R. Rother

EAST SUSSEX

R. Adur

Battle

Rye

CHICHESTER

Arundel

LEWES

R. Ouse

Hastings

West Wittering

Selsey

Bognor Regis

Littlehampton

Worthing

BRIGHTON

Newhaven

R. Cuckmere

Bexhill

Pevensey

Eastbourne

N
W — E
S

0   10   20   30   40

Scale: km

COASTAL PLAIN
SOUTH DOWNS
WESTERN HILL COUNTRY
EASTERN LEVELS
LOW WEALD
HIGH WEALD

INTRODUCTION

This book has become a homecoming. A nostalgic return to many of the most beautiful and interesting areas of this warm, mellow county, a county where my own roots have run deep since early childhood. Sussex is possibly the best known of all seaside counties, 'a comfortable size for a comfortable county' in the words of Ian Nairn, and containing a remarkable variety of features and scenery within its 120km breadth from Thorney to Camber. Often described as the most English of counties, Sussex can almost be defined by the fresh salty tang of the sea air, the soft, gentle expanse and wide views of Kipling's 'whale backed' South Downs or the 'blue goodness' of the distant Weald.

There are many who would say that Sussex has it all; from the busy, sunny promenades and elegant terraces of Brighton and Eastbourne to the drama of the white chalk cliffs of the Seven Sisters; from the dusty, homely flint Downland villages to the medieval hammer ponds lying still and silent in the depths of the Wealden valleys. There is the evidence of Neolithic man on Cissbury Ring and The Trundle, the Romans at Bignor and Fishbourne, the Saxon church masterpieces of Bosham, Sompting and Worth and, of course, Battle, associated with the single date in English history when the fate of a nation was decided, 1066.

The Normans left their imprint on many of the county's great buildings; the medieval oak-framed hall houses of the Weald testify to the short-lived prosperity of the Sussex iron industry; whilst many of the streets of Chichester appear almost as they did after the great 'rebuilding' of the Georgian era. From the heights of Blackdown to the fertile coastal plain or from the fringes of Romney Marsh to the wilds of Ashdown Forest, there is much to be seen and loved. It is a county of tremendous, yet harmonious contrasts, a county of an inexhaustible richness in both its heritage and physical geography.

Sussex attracts enormous crowds to its seaside resorts in summer when often the Downs are dotted with more walkers and cyclists than the once ubiquitous South Downs sheep. Yet there are places where one can still steal away for solitude, amongst the deep, sunken lanes and tracks of the hill country around Midhurst and Petworth or the rifes of the Manhood Peninsula. In winter the beaches are often deserted of all human life and the silence of the High Wealden ridges is broken only by the drone of an occasional aircraft from Gatwick.

Moods of Sussex, aspects or features of Sussex perhaps! The Oxford English Dictionary defines the word 'mood' as a 'state of mind or feeling' and it is this 'feeling' for Sussex and its history that I have tried to incorporate within my photographs and text.

Mood can be a fleeting, glancing shaft of sunlight on a Downland hillside or an almost indefinable spirit in the depths of Battle's undercrofts. It can be the 'Kiss me Quick' of a summer's afternoon on the 'prom' or the song of a skylark over Firle Beacon. From the quiet, drifting morning mists of the Arun valley to the roar of the crowds at Goodwood Races, mood can be interpreted in so many different ways. Within these pages are just a few of the many moods of a much loved county – Sussex by the Sea.

There ant no place like Sussex
Until you goos Above,
But Sussex will be Sussex
And Sussex won't be Druv!

W. Victor Cook: *Sussex Won't be Druv*

A glorious early summer's day at Brighton looking down on to the lower promenade. The beach, blue skies, sun hats, coloured umbrellas, ice cream, striped deck chairs – everything one could wish of an English seaside resort. Guide books from an earlier era quoted 'the salubrity of the air, the excellent quality of the water, the pleasing healthful and convenient situation of the town ... and many other advantages both of nature and art give Brighthelmstone a superiority to the other watering places'. In many ways the statement still applies today and Brighton is generally regarded as the premier seaside resort in Britain. Only the fire-blackened, storm-ravaged, skeletal remains of the old West Pier in the background mar the scene.

Brighton, the coastal resorts
and
SUSSEX BY THE SEA

Brighton Rock in its many colours. Think of Sussex and probably the first words that come to mind are the closing lines of Kipling's unofficial anthem entitled 'Sussex' 'yea Sussex by the sea'. Sussex throughout its history has always depended on the sea and to this day it is possibly best known for its string of coastal resorts that have in many ways become a part of our language and national institutions. Sea bathing started as a fashionable pastime during the early years of the eighteenth century, the coastal towns and villages gradually developing as holiday and health resorts following the pattern of inland spa towns. Doctors and physicians began sending patients to the coast for the seawater's curative and restorative powers and with the publication in 1752 of Dr Richard Russell's *Dissertation Concerning the use of Seawater in Diseases of the Glands,* together with the arrival of the railways from the 1840s onwards, the Sussex seaside resorts were born. Brighton's ranking as 'Queen of the Watering Places' has never been seriously challenged in Sussex but the resorts of Bexhill, Bognor Regis, Eastbourne, Hastings, Littlehampton and Worthing have aspired to at least a certain degree of imitation over the succeeding years.

Restored bathing machine, Eastbourne. The invention of the bathing machine in the first half of the eighteenth century encouraged many visitors to the seaside resorts. Comprising a decorated hut on wheels and with stairs at both ends, it enabled prospective bathers to enter at one end from the beach, undress in total privacy and then descend into the water from the other end, sometimes with assistance. The machines were simply moved up or down the beach according to the tides. This machine, now in the care of the Langham Hotel, is possibly the only surviving example of the many thousands of similar machines once seen on the Sussex shores.

Brighton Pier at dusk. Seaside piers were constructed initially to serve packet boats and pleasure steamers but soon became popular with promenaders, enabling them to 'walk the waters' without feeling seasick! Brighton Pier, previously known as the Palace Pier, was the third to be built in the town (after the Chain and West Piers), opening in 1899 and described as 'the grandest pier ever built'. Its pleasure facilities included shops, a theatre and a concert hall. During its lifetime many changes have been made to keep up with modern-day trends and this 'palace of fun' is still one of Brighton's chief tourist attractions. Piers were also built at Bognor Regis, Eastbourne, Hastings and Worthing.

Seaside architecture. **Opposite:** Royal Crescent, Brighton, built between 1798 and 1807 and described by Pevsner as 'the earliest unified composition of Brighton'. This series of houses was the forerunner of the Regency squares and terraces, constructed for wealthy visitors and residents, that have given Brighton and Hove much of its architectural charm. **Above:** The rhythm of Brunswick Terrace, Hove, overlooking the lawns and promenade and built as part of the self-contained Brunswick estate between 1825 and 1828.

The Royal Pavilion, Brighton. Transformed from a more modest residence into a grand palace for George, then Prince Regent and eldest son of King George III, and completed in 1822 after a number of his years being spent at Brighton, the amazing oriental extravagance known as the Royal Pavilion is Brighton's best known building. With its pagoda roofs, minarets, colonnades and onion shaped domes, it has also one of the most recognisable profiles in Britain. Following George's death in 1830 as King George IV, the building was for a short period still used as a royal residence. However, the estate was transferred to the town in 1850, and the palace was then opened to the public. Its now restored exotic decoration and furnishings are still a popular attraction.

Bandstand concert, Eastbourne. One of the most popular attractions along Eastbourne seafront is the series of open-air bandstand concerts performed almost daily over the summer season by various local and visiting brass and concert bands. Special events are also held including Rock 'n Roll nights, Proms nights and firework concerts. The bandstand itself, constructed in Art-Deco style, was completed in 1935 and is regarded as one of the finest in the country for the quality of acoustics. Eastbourne Pier is in the background. In 1813 Eastbourne was noted as a small fashionable watering place but it was not until the 1850s on the initiative of the 7th Duke of Devonshire that major development began. Eastbourne's three-tier promenade backed by landscaped gardens, elegant hotels and large private houses is a notable feature of this distinguished resort.

Lower Promenade, Brighton. It was this stretch of beach below the old town that was used by the early sea bathers in the 1730s and increasingly so after Dr Richard Russell's dissertation on the use of seawater. Brighton's once large fishing fleet was also kept on the beach in this vicinity and the nearby Fishing Museum charts the town's earlier importance before its resort status. Brighton, often known as London by the Sea, was even by the 1780s the nation's premier seaside resort and one of the fastest growing towns in England. Now designated a city, it is still a place of spectacular contrasts, culture and colour.

Eating in the sun, alfresco style, The Lanes, Brighton. Brighton's old town or 'The Lanes' as it is known today comprises a dense patchwork of what were at one time cramped fishermen's and tradesmen's houses and businesses dating back to the seventeenth and eighteenth centuries. Now converted into colourful small shops, fashion outlets, pubs, cafés and restaurants, the area has become a world-famous tourist attraction, with a network of narrow winding alleys, footways and small squares. Shoppers, artists, diners and buskers abound.

Bowls tournament, Worthing. Once a small fishing village, Worthing developed initially as a small-scale version of Brighton only later expanding to become one of the largest towns in Sussex. With its 6km promenade and pier, it is still one of the most popular resorts in the county with all-year attractions including the National Bowls Championships held annually in Beach House Park.

Seaside colour, Bognor Regis. Despite early schemes, Bognor did not develop until the 1820s, again in imitation of the larger seaside resorts, but in an extremely piecemeal fashion. A contemporary account describes 'several rows of elegant brick structures, but so detached ... erected with the professed design of making Bognor the resort of more select company than is to be found at other bathing places'. The town still has a curiously disjointed character and as late as the 1930s considered itself superior to other Sussex resorts. The word 'Regis' was bestowed after King George V's convalescence there in 1929. The King's classic remark 'Bugger Bognor' occurred later when asked if he wished to make a return visit!

Seafront souvenirs, Brighton, Littlehampton and Worthing.

Seafront advertising, Camber Sands. Camber Sands stretch eastwards from the mouth of the River Rother at Rye Harbour almost to the Kent/Sussex border. As the largest open sand beach in Sussex, it is backed by high dunes and is over 1km broad at low tide – a paradise for building sand castles. Camber itself however has been described as 'a haphazard collection of bungalows, shacks and shanties' perhaps exemplified by this style of advertising.

West Wittering Beach. The unspoilt sandy beach at West Wittering, close to East Head and the entrance to Chichester Harbour, has been popular with bathers since the 1920s and more recently with windsurfers. For a number of years it has been classed as the best beach in the United Kingdom, regularly receiving clean beach and water quality awards. This is a crowded scene on a hot August afternoon.

Empty sands, East Head. Despite the often-crowded beaches in summer at West Wittering, neighbouring East Head can equally be enjoyed in winter without another soul in sight. The quickly-changing tides and light give a totally different atmosphere of space and peace. This view looks out to sea and the distant Isle of Wight. Hayling Island is on the right and West Wittering just out of the picture on the left.

Clearing skies, Worthing. The beach, totally devoid of any visitors, slowly dries out after a night's rain. Worthing Pier is in the background.

Winter promenade, Hove. The wide promenade, built at the end of the nineteenth century along the length of Hove seafront, is a highly popular venue for strolling, jogging, cycling, roller blading or just watching the world go by from one of the many cafés along its length. Even in the worst of winter conditions there are always a few hardy souls to be found here.

Just landed.

Hastings. **Above:** The tall, thin, weather-boarded and gable-roofed net shops clustered along The Stade close to the old town. These distinctive structures, possibly originating in Tudor times, are almost totally unique to Hastings and used for storage of fishermen's tackle and hanging nets.

Hastings Pier built in 1872.

Old Town, Hastings. The historic old town of Hastings nestling below two ridges and stretching down to the sea dates back to the fourteenth century and is a fascinating contrast to what is principally a Victorian resort with a few Regency survivals. Consisting of the parallel High Street and All Saints Street, reached and linked by numerous narrow lanes, passages and alleyways, the old town presents a remarkable variety of almost unspoilt domestic architecture from different periods and styles. From the hills above, the colours and forms of the crowded roofs take on a patchwork appearance. Hastings has always had close connections with the sea, being one of the original Cinque Ports with a large fishing fleet and one of the few coastal towns left in Sussex where fishing is still active to some degree. The Cinque Ports were a confederation of certain Sussex and Kent coastal towns and villages that obtained privileges from the monarchy in early medieval times in exchange for supplying ships for the nation's defence.

Camera Obscura, Eastbourne. This board advertises the camera obscura on Eastbourne Pier and some of its history. The revolving camera shows panoramic views of the surrounding scene, projected by natural light using a mirror and lens, on to a circular screen situated within the dome. This technology dates back to the sixteenth century. Before moving pictures were commonly available, camera obscuras were the only way to see real-life moving images. They are now very rare, and few are open to the public.

Beachy Head. Immediately west of Eastbourne, the cliffs rise steeply to a height of 163m at Beachy Head, the highest chalk cliffs on the south coast and one of the most famous landmarks in England. The prominent red and white lighthouse below was completed in 1902, much of the labour and materials needed being lowered via an aerial ropeway from the top of the cliffs. On top of the head is the original Belle Tout lighthouse built in 1831 and now used as a private residence. Built from Aberdeen granite this structure was recently moved back some distance from the crumbling cliff edge and the dangers of erosion.

The Seven Sisters from below Birling Gap. From Beachy Head westwards, as the South Downs meet the sea, the perpendicular white cliffs stretch in an undulating wall for almost 8 km to Cuckmere Haven. Known as the Seven Sisters they form one of the most dramatic sections of unspoilt coastline remaining in Britain. Along the top the South Downs Way long-distance bridlepath starts its journey from Eastbourne to Winchester. At Birling Gap, a hotel and a few houses still brave the ever-receding cliffs crumbling at an average of over half a metre each year. Cliff falls are common especially after a sharp frost. Birling Gap also provides the only access to the beaches below the cliffs via a stepped walkway.

The Seven Sisters from Seaford Head. Undoubtedly one of the most distinctive views in Sussex and possibly in Great Britain, almost the entire length of the Seven Sisters cliffs can be seen, ranging from Haven Brow along to Went Hill Brow with the old Belle Tout lighthouse in the far distance. On the left the Cuckmere valley, one of the few undeveloped estuaries remaining along the south coast and now part of the Seven Sisters Country Park, reaches the sea.

Chichester Cathedral. Part of the magnificent window in the South Transept built in the decorative style in about 1330 by Bishop John De Langton. He was Chancellor of England and is buried beneath the window. The stained glass was installed later. The Norman cathedral church of the Holy Trinity was built on the site of a Saxon church and the east end was dedicated in 1108. Twice requiring reconstruction during the same century due to fire damage, the building was finally completed, including cloisters and bell tower, in 1420. The spire, the third tallest in England, was rebuilt between 1861 and 1866 after a disastrous collapse. The Cathedral is unique in not only having a detached bell tower but also being the only cathedral which can be seen from the sea. Pevsner has described the building as 'one of the most lovable of English cathedrals – a well worn, well loved, comfortable fireside chair of a cathedral'.

Chichester
and
THE COASTAL PLAIN

The Cathedral with St Richard's Walk. St Richard's Walk leads from the cloisters to the area of the Close containing the Bishop's Palace, Chantry and Deanery.

Chichester, the county town of West Sussex and one of England's smallest cities was founded during the Roman occupation as Noviomagus Regnensium although evidence abounds of man's earlier existence in the area. Acknowledged to be one of the premier Roman towns in Britain, the city's main streets are still based on the original Roman plan and much of the 2½km Roman walls constructed in the third century and later rebuilt in the medieval period are still in existence. There was once a Norman castle but this was destroyed during the thirteenth century. Becoming an important port and market town, the city enjoyed a major period of prosperity during the seventeenth, eighteenth and nineteenth centuries and many of its outstanding Georgian buildings still in existence were remodelled or constructed at this time. Now a rapidly-growing heritage and tourist destination, the city has been voted one of the most ideal locations to live in the country, reflecting its considerable importance in Sussex and Southern England.

Chichester Festival Theatre. In recent years Chichester has built up an enviable reputation as a centre for arts and culture with its annual Chichester Festivities and the internationally famous Festival Theatre. The theatre, opened in 1962 and first directed by Laurence Olivier, was constructed to a hexagonal design with an open stage and was later joined by the adjacent smaller Minerva Theatre complex. With a proud record of many outstanding productions, the Festival Theatre is now regarded as one of the leading venues for provincial theatregoers.

The Market Cross, seen here from West Street in front of the Cathedral, acts as the city's focal point where the four main streets meet. Built in 1501, it was a place where the poorer tradesmen could sell their goods free from local taxes. Considerably repaired and restored over the years and with its original use being declared redundant due to the moving of the market, it is now difficult to believe that it was circumnavigated by twentieth-century traffic until pedestrianisation of the main streets in the 1970s. Today the cross has become a popular meeting place and backdrop for busking musicians and local events.

Despite its small size, Chichester is outstandingly rich in architectural heritage and detail. Much of the city was transformed during the eighteenth and early nineteenth centuries with many fine buildings erected, giving rise to it being regarded as a 'Georgian' city. This is a small selection of the wealth of Georgian door cases and fanlights that can be discovered here.

Pallant House was built in 1712, a particularly fine example of Chichester's Georgian architecture, constructed to a high standard of craftsmanship both inside and out. At the time of building it cost £3000, an enormous sum of money for the period. It is now open as an historic house and art gallery. The four streets of the Pallants reflect the city's main street plan in miniature and are still lined with many elegant buildings of the Georgian era.

Roman mosaic floor, Fishbourne. The flat, fertile coastal plain extends from the foot of the South Downs to the coast and stretches from the Hampshire border in the west tapering off to the River Adur on the outskirts of Brighton in the east. Within this area are the various tidal inlets, channels and creeks that form Chichester Harbour, the possible route for the Roman invasion of the district. At the head of the harbour lies Fishbourne and it was here in 1961 that the largest known Roman domestic building north of the Alps was discovered. Within the foundations of this four-winged palace were the remains of more than 20 mosaic floors and 'the Cupid on a Dolphin' shown here is the most striking. The site, now fully protected and including a Roman plant display area, has become a leading museum receiving several million visitors since its opening to the public in 1968. At Bignor, north of the Downs, the substantial remains of a Roman villa were found in 1811, including further mosaic flooring, and this too is now a museum.

An almost timeless scene of the thirteenth-century church of St Mary the Virgin at Apuldram, situated on the edge of the harbour near Fishbourne, in thick mist. Apuldram is a shrunken medieval village that at one time contained a quay servicing ships sailing up the Fishbourne channel.

Early morning light, Dell Quay. During the middle ages, Chichester and its harbour was considered to be a major port. Cargoes were shipped to Dell Quay and then transferred by wagon to the city itself, which is not on the sea. This laborious system ceased on completion of the Chichester branch of the Portsmouth to Arundel Canal, that sadly closed in 1906. Dell Quay therefore was a major factor in the city's prosperity, but today recreational sailing is the main activity. This view from the quay looks north up the Fishbourne channel at high tide to the distant South Downs. Chichester Harbour is rich in wild life, particularly sea birds and waders and is of considerable historical significance.

Late afternoon sunshine at Chichester Yacht Basin. Chichester Harbour extends to some 30 square kilometres of inter-tidal waters and almost 30 kilometres of navigable channels. It is therefore an ideal area for recreational sailing with several marinas, sailing clubs and associations, sailing schools, activity centres and boat yards. Chichester Yacht Basin is often host to several thousand craft at any one time.

Bosham from across Bosham channel. Bosham was an important Saxon settlement and the tower of the beautiful Holy Trinity Church, with its outstanding chancel arch, dates from this period. The church appears on the Bayeux Tapestry in connection with Harold's ill-fated visit to Normandy in 1064, two years before the Norman invasion. The village has for centuries been known for its shipbuilding but now, regarded as the most attractive village around the harbour, it is a popular tourist and sailing haunt.

Winter emptiness at East Head. Chichester Harbour reaches the sea at East Head opposite Eastoke Point on Hayling Island. Here the vast tidal sands and flats are a popular paddling area for summer visitors, hopefully wary of the treacherous tides. In winter it is generally deserted. East Head itself, a raised sandy spit of some 50ha, is now in severe danger due to erosion. This is a factor which may have important consequences for the harbour's well-being in future years.

Fallen leaves, West Dean Gardens. The gardens surround West Dean House, a flint mansion to the north of Chichester near the foot of the Downs, once owned by Edward James the poet and major patron of the arts. Following the establishment of the Edward James Foundation, the house became a college specialising in traditional arts, crafts, conservation and restoration techniques and its gardens were opened to the public. In addition to the formal ornamental gardens with many exotic trees, there are water and wild gardens, pergolas, a 100ha landscaped park, arboretum and the award-winning restored Edwardian kitchen garden with its numerous glasshouses, frames and visitor centre. Each year special events are held celebrating a variety of fruits and vegetables.

Boxgrove Priory. The Benedictine Priory of Boxgrove is one of the county's most important ecclesiastical buildings. Founded in the twelfth century, it was dissolved in 1537, leaving only the priory church of St Mary and St Blaise for the villagers to worship in. The beautiful interior is noted for its vaulted painted ceiling of intertwined heraldry and foliage dating from the sixteenth century and the highly decorative De la Warr Chantry, the only complete chantry chapel in Sussex. The ruins of the priory guesthouse can be found outside the church.

The coastal plain is at its broadest where the shoreline curves south to Selsey Bill, the southernmost point of what is known as the Manhood Peninsula. Being almost entirely flat, the land is drained by a network of rifes and ditches interspersed by isolated farms and hamlets and narrow winding lanes. It feels in places more like Lincolnshire than West Sussex and despite its proximity to Chichester it is still relatively unknown to many people. This is Pagham Rife, one of the principal outlets of the Chichester Flood Relief Scheme, near North Honer Farm with its willow-lined banks in early summer.

Crop planting, South Mundham. One of the principal features of the Manhood Peninsula is the sense of openness with vast skies and wide horizons. With its fertile soils, long hours of sunshine and high quality of light, the area has become extremely popular for intensive horticultural production. Many modern farming techniques and unusual crops are found and this picture of maize planting near South Mundham gives an almost surreal aspect to the landscape.

Intensive horticulture, Runcton. Much of the intensive horticulture on the coastal plain is now carried out within extensive modern automated glasshouses. These are mainly used for the production of cucumbers, herbs, lettuces, peppers, tomatoes and other salad crops and fresh food produce, cut and potted flowers and bedding plants. Forming a paving-like pattern, these are young lettuce plants in the hardening area of Madestein UK's nursery near Runcton.

Pumpkin display, Slindon. This colourful display features just a small number of the many pumpkins and squashes that are on sale at Mr and Mrs Upton's cottage and adjacent yard at Slindon. Every year, before Halloween, during the months of September and October a new thematic display is produced when the vegetables are brought from nearby glasshouses to be sold. Over 30 varieties are grown and the Upton's reputation has grown with them, with television interviews and numerous articles written in lifestyle magazines, newspapers, supplements and recipe books by and about this enterprising couple and their family helpers.

Norman doorway, Climping. The church of St Mary at Climping is known particularly for the outstanding Norman architectural details on the lower half of its tower. Surrounding the tower's west door and lancet window above is the most amazing set of stone mouldings, carved in undercut, rolled, zig-zag, dog-tooth and chevron designs and a complete contrast to the more severe style of the rest of the building which dates from a slightly later period. An old West Sussex saying about churches describes ' Bosham for antiquity, Boxgrove for beauty and Climping for perfection.'

Within the graveyard of the church of St Mary at nearby Walberton is this interesting headstone to Charles Cook. He was killed by a falling tree and the woodman is shown holding up his hand in despair. Death, time, angels, scales of justice and God are all featured.

Arundel Castle. A view of Arundel Castle from the banks of the River Arun on a cold, misty winters' morning. Arundel from a distance has one of the most dramatic skylines in England with its castle and cathedral high up on a ridge, backed by the Downs and with the town laid out below. The castle itself, the ancestral home of the Dukes of Norfolk, mainly dates from an almost total rebuilding between 1890 and 1903 with some earlier additions and Norman and medieval ruins from the eleventh to thirteenth centuries remaining from the civil war. Built in a style not dissimilar to Windsor Castle, it is impressive simply by its bulk and situation and is a highly popular visitor attraction.

With its vast pile of round and square towers reaching to the sky, the Gothic-styled castle not only dominates the town but also the park and countryside around. Arundel park of some 500 hectares stretches north into the West Sussex countryside with glorious views over the Downs and a favourite location for walkers and horse riding. The attractive small town of closely-knit period houses, built on the side of a hill and reaching down to the river, has become a major centre for the antiques trade and the venue for the annual Arundel Arts Festival.

Carpet of Flowers, Arundel Cathedral. The Catholic Cathedral Church of Our Lady and St Philip Howard was completed in 1873, built by the 15th Duke of Norfolk to commemorate his coming of age. Situated at the very top of the town, its imposing outline seems more French than English. In late spring the celebration of Corpus Christi is held, the largest in the country and with it the associated floral festival and carpet of flowers within the Cathedral. The theme for the carpet of flowers changes each year and the fresh flowers themselves are laid out in their thousands by many willing volunteers down the centre aisle of the Cathedral. Here they remain for two days on display. The photograph shows the formation of the carpet taking place for the 2005 celebration.

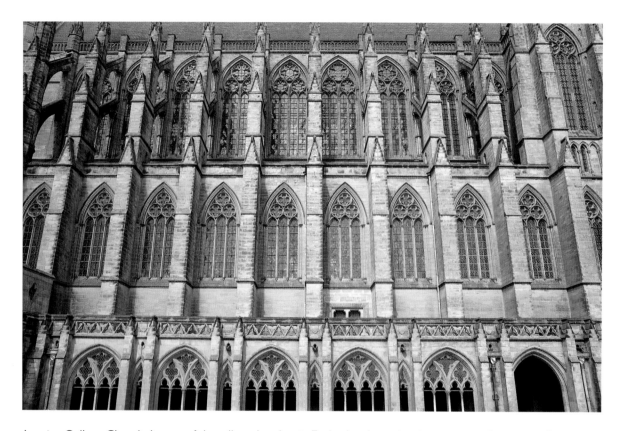

Lancing College Chapel. As one of the tallest churches in England and a national monument, the spectacular soaring Gothic chapel built for the Woodard School of Lancing College was begun in 1868. The construction continued until the present structure was completed in 1911, long after the death of the original architect R. C. Carpenter and Nathaniel Woodard himself. An intended north tower and west end has never been built. The chapel with its almost 30m high interior is situated on a sloping, exposed site high up next to the school overlooking the Downs and the Adur valley and required foundations of some 20m in depth. Nathaniel Woodard's aim was to found a comprehensive and classless federation of schools independent of the state system of which Lancing, Ardingly and Hurstpierpoint (all in Sussex) are three out of a total of 20.

Afternoon calm, Shoreham Harbour. As the Downs reach the sea, the coastal plain finishes at Shoreham and the mouth of the River Adur. With a long history of silting and changes in direction (and the subsequent rebuilding of Shoreham itself), a new outlet to the sea was cut for the navigable River Adur in 1818. The former riverbed towards Brighton was then slowly transformed into a busy harbour by the construction of a lock enabling vessels to berth at any tide. Now one of the busiest small ports in the country, a considerable variety of materials including food products, are handled and a number of new marinas have been developed. Newhaven and Littlehampton are the other significant ports in Sussex.

A misty, early October morning view from Bury Hill looking down to the Arun valley. The South Downs have had many associations with well-known writers over the centuries and it was near here that John Galsworthy lived at Bury House. After his death his ashes were scattered on Bury Hill. The mist hanging in the valley and swirling around the trees is a common sight during the autumn and winter months in this part of West Sussex.

Lewes
and
THE SOUTH DOWNS

A sense of infinity. The Downs near Amberley Mount. The South Downs stretch in an almost straight line across the county from the Hampshire border to Eastbourne, a distance of some 90km. Further west they continue to the outskirts of Hampshire's historical city of Winchester. Broken only by the valleys of the Rivers Arun, Adur, Ouse and Cuckmere within Sussex, they form one of the most well-known and loved landscape features in Great Britain. Hillaire Belloc once wrote

When I am living in the Midlands
That are sodden and unkind .....
The great hills of the South Country
Come back into my mind.

It is above all on the South Downs that the spirit of Sussex lies, in their green expanse and wide views to both coast and the inland weald. The skies, the air and the song of the skylark are the essence of these softly-rounded chalk hills where surviving Iron Age hillforts, circular burial tumuli and downland trackways still remind us of five thousand years of Sussex history.

The Downs near Goodwood. The scene looking north towards the village of Singleton from the Trundle. This latter hill with its Iron-Age hillfort ramparts commands spectacular views in all directions including the Goodwood Race Course and the distant city of Chichester on the coastal plain.

Summer skies and poppies. Looking across open fields to the Trundle. The naturalist Gilbert White wrote in 1773, 'Though I have now travelled the South Downs upwards of thirty years, yet I still investigate that chain of majestic mountains with fresh admiration year by year; and think I see new beauties every time I traverse it!'

Winter snow on Bignor Hill with Amberley Mount, the Arun valley, the Amberley Wild Brooks wetlands and much of the West Sussex Downs in the distance. The South Downs Way passes by here. This long distance bridleway was the first in the country to be designated by the former Countryside Commission in 1972. It is a highly popular recreational route for walkers, cyclists and horse riders and now stretches from Eastbourne 160km to Winchester in Hampshire. The Wild Brooks, an area of dyke-drained pasture and scrub provided grazing and hay for farmers' livestock for centuries. In winter they are often completely flooded whilst in summer they are a haven for insects, birds, flowers and wetland plant species.

Barn interior, Upwaltham. This timber-framed barn is typical of so many similar structures to be found all over the Downs. Convenient local materials such as brick, flint, stone, timber and clunch were commonly used and the barns sited where needed. Varying considerably in size, some barns were little more than crude shelters whilst others such as the 52m long tithe barn at Alciston were magnificent buildings, often in monastic ownership.

Uppark House. Of all the many grand country houses situated within the South Downs, Uppark is one of the finest and best known. Enjoying dramatic views to the Isle of Wight from high on the Downs above South Harting, the house was built about 1690, later being remodelled by the Fetherstonhaugh family at various times. It was furnished in grand fashion reflecting their travels around the world and in this condition remained unaltered from the mid nineteenth century until the disastrous fire in 1989 which totally gutted the interior. After the fire the National Trust, who by then owned the property, took the brave decision to return the house to its original pre-fire condition, this being finally achieved when Uppark was re-opened to visitors in 1995 after a remarkable restoration programme.

Oilseed rape fields on the slopes of Bury Hill. This is just one of the more colourful crops now to be found on the South Downs and often referred to as England's Yellow Peril since it is such a distinctive feature of the rural landscape in late spring.

Whilst much of the East Sussex Downs are generally devoid of trees, the West Sussex Downs, especially west of Bignor, are in places well wooded. This is Wildham Wood near Stoughton with a carpet of bluebells and ramsons in early spring. Nearby Kingley Vale, a national nature reserve, contains the finest yew forest in Europe.

The interior of the thirteenth-century church of St Michael, Up Marden. Not far from
Stoughton and situated in a remote hamlet high up on the West Sussex Downs, this church
has been described by Pevsner as having 'one of the loveliest interiors in England. With
an atmosphere as tangible as any moulding, the slow, loving, gentle accretion century
by century until it is something as organic as any of the South Downs views around it.
A visible loving testimony of the faith of successive generations.'

Norman arches, St Andrew's Church, Steyning. This beautiful Norman church is built on the site of an earlier Saxon timber structure and reflects Steyning's then importance as a seaport on the River Adur. The building has been referred to as 'the most majestic fragment of twelfth century ecclesiastical architecture in Sussex' and 'among the best in the whole country'. Although the Norman tower, crossing and choir were demolished after the reformation, the outstanding Romanesque nave was left intact with its magnificent richly-carved arches to both north and south aisles and chancel and massive supporting cylindrical piers. It is known that King Ethelwulf, the father of King Alfred, was buried in the original Saxon church so one of the two surviving Saxon coffin lids on display in the present building could perhaps have covered his grave.

Church Street, Steyning. Steyning was an established settlement by the time of the Domesday Book and known for a short while as St Cuthman's Port after the saint who founded its original Saxon church. The surviving buildings in Church Street, built between the fifteenth and seventeenth centuries reflect Steyning's growth in the Middle Ages and the old Grammar School, on the left of the photograph, founded in 1614 still incorporates sections of an earlier timber-framed guildhall.

Parascending on Dyke Hill. The hill and the deep curving valley of the nearby Devil's Dyke have been famous beauty spots for many years. At one time a railway branch line terminated here from Brighton, an aerial cableway spanned the dyke and a funicular railway constructed on the northern slope of Dyke Hill ascended from near Poynings. In the late nineteenth century these, together with a thriving hotel on the summit, would often attract up to 30,000 visitors to the area on Bank Holidays. The hill is now popular for hang gliding and parascending with a good source of suitable up-lifting air currents. Fulking can be seen below and Chanctonbury Ring, behind Worthing, can be discerned in the far distance.

Jack and Jill windmills, Clayton. Probably the most famous windmills in Sussex and a notable sight for passengers travelling by train to Brighton, these windmills stand high on the Downs not far from Ditchling Beacon. Jack, the furthest in the photograph, is a painted, brick-built tower mill constructed in the late 1890s, its cap and sweeps being able to turn and face the wind. Jill, a white painted timber post mill, relies on its entire structure revolving around a massive wooden pillar to suit the wind direction. Jill was originally built about 1820 near Brighton and later dismantled and moved to its present site in the mid nineteenth century, hauled across the Downs by teams of oxen. At 248m, Ditchling Beacon is the highest point on the East Sussex Downs and one of the sites where fires were lit to warn of the Armada four centuries ago.

The Barbican, Lewes Castle. Lewes, county town of East Sussex, lies in and around a hollow of the Downs where the River Ouse passes through on its way to the sea. That this was a naturally strategic position was soon realised by the Normans after the conquest and a castle was commenced by William de Warenne in about 1100 on a ridge overlooking the river. Originally comprising two shell keeps on individual mounds, only the western keep has survived and still dominates the town. The flint and stone Barbican (outer gateway) was added in the fourteenth century, the last section of the castle to be built and is regarded as one of the finest in England. It incorporated all the then state-of-the-art defensive features such as drawbridge, gates, portcullis, arrow loops and machicolations. Castlegate House can be seen through the archway.

The town is notable for its variety of architecture and its history as a port and administrative centre. The lanes, 'twittens' and pedestrian alleys that drop from the High Street to the lower town probably date from the planning of Lewes as a Saxon stronghold by King Alfred.

Right: Buildings in St Anne's Hill leading down to the High Street and dating from the Georgian period back to the fifteenth century.

Above: A plaque to the Lewes physician Dr Richard Russell who practised medicine in the town.

Left: Houses in the steeply graded Keere Street.

Left: Some of the remaining fragments of the Cluniac Priory of St Pancras founded in 1077 and largely destroyed by Thomas Cromwell in 1538. This was thought to be one of the most magnificent monasteries ever built in this country.

Below: The colourful gardens of Southover Grange. The Grange was built in 1572 using Caen stone from the demolished Priory. John Evelyn the horticulturist and diarist once lived here.

Below left: Anne of Cleves House, a timber-framed sixteenth-century Wealden hall house once belonging to Henry VIII's fourth wife and now open as a museum.

Lewes has become a prominent centre for antiques and second-hand books in recent years. This bookshop window is part of the '15th Century Bookshop' in the High Street. A milestone giving the distance from Cornhill in London is set in the jettied timber framing above. The town has also become well known for its traditional celebrations on Guy Fawkes night which the numerous bonfire societies commemorate with great enthusiasm. Seventeen Protestant martyrs were burned at the stake here between 1555 and 1557 as part of the campaign to re-establish the authority of the Pope, and 5 November is used to remember the Lewes Martyrs as well as Guy Fawkes.

Downland sheep. A part of the window installed in the Gage family sepulchral chapel of the church of St Peter, Firle. Designed by John Piper and entitled 'Homage to William Blake's Book of Job', the window depicts 'the tree of life' in the heavenly Jerusalem and features sheep from which the Southdown breed were developed in the late eighteenth century. The window was completed in 1985 in memory of the 6th Viscount Gage, Henry Rainald KCVO, who held the title for seventy years and died in 1982. Southdown sheep were famous for their superb quality wool and cleanliness and formed the basis of much breeding stock used worldwide. Today they have generally been replaced by the shaggy cross-bred providing a more desirable meat.

Sheep and winter show. During the early years of the nineteenth century, figures have been quoted of up to a quarter of a million ewes grazing on the Downs between Eastbourne and Steyning. A century later this ancient method of land management had begun to give way to planted crops and today it is reckoned that at least 95% of the old chalk grasslands have disappeared. For possibly more complicated reasons, it is also becoming less common to receive heavy snowfalls in Sussex.

A glorious spring day on the Downs near Firle Beacon looking inland towards Charleston Farm and Kipling's 'wooded dim blue goodness of the Weald'. Note the numerous cowslips in flower, these slowly becoming abundant once again on many of the Downland slopes.

Charleston Farm. Often known as Bloomsbury in Sussex, the seventeenth-century Charleston Farm was the home of the painters Clive and Vanessa Bell and Duncan Grant from about 1916 onwards. Here an artistic, somewhat emotional, unconventional and bohemian partnership flourished where the farmhouse fabric was literally transformed into a colourful canvas containing painted works, fabrics, pottery etc. Over the years the farm became a favourite retreat for others of the Bloomsbury set and now forms an important part of twentieth-century artistic heritage. In recent years the house has been carefully restored by the Charleston Trust together with the adjoining painters' and traditional English cottage gardens and is open to the public. Vanessa's sister, the writer Virginia Wolfe, lived nearby at Monks House in Rodmell.

'Underhill lane' near Alciston. Below the steeper northern scarp slope of much of the Downs, narrow underhill lanes follow the course of ancient trackways used over the last two thousand or so years to serve farmsteads, churches, small villages, hamlets and fortified locations. Sometimes shrouded by trees, sometimes caked in chalk and set between deep banks or sometimes simply open to the elements, these winding and undulating lanes and byways still form a living history where the years can be counted by the number of plant species in the hedgerows and where the words of Philip Larkin come to mind from his poem *Cut Grass*: 'White lilac bowed, lost lanes of Queen Anne's lace, and that high builded cloud moving at Summer's pace'. This particular lane between Berwick and West Firle is known as the old coach road, once used by eighteenth-century stagecoaches to Eastbourne before the building of the present A27.

Evocative Downland textures during different seasons of the year.

The flint church of St Peter at Southease is one of only three Sussex churches built with a round tower, the others being St Michael at Lewes and St John at Piddinghoe further down the Ouse valley. Having contracted in size over the years by the loss of its aisles and chancel, possibly due to the Black Death, the church nevertheless celebrated 1000 years of recorded history in 1966. In a sense this story is typical of so many of these small, almost timeless, Downland churches supported simply by isolated hamlets or shrinking villages. Simon Jenkins in his *England's Thousand Best Churches* states 'the churches of the Sussex Downs merit a book to themselves. They are the simplest religious structures in England, begun by pious Saxons and Normans and mostly left alone in their poverty even by the Victorians'.

Cuckmere valley. The view from High and Over looking down on to the winding snake-like River Cuckmere as it flows its last few kilometres to the sea at Cuckmere Haven. The popular village of Alfriston lies just out of the photograph and to where the river was once navigable. Nearby Exceat Bridge preserves the name of a long vanished Saxon village.

The Long Man of Wilmington. A Sussex mystery! The 73m-high Long Man with a staff in each hand cut out of the chalk Downland of Windover Hill near Alfriston remains an enigma of uncertain age and purpose. He is possibly the largest outline of a human figure in Europe and undoubtedly the most well known of the chalk hill images in England. His history could go back 5000 years but his present stark appearance dates back only to the late nineteenth century, based on investigations by Dr J. S. Phenè and now outlined within the chalk by white blocks. It is thought that originally he might have been holding a rake in one hand and a scythe in the other but this too is only conjecture.

From the Wilmington to Alfriston road, one obtains this classic view of the East Sussex Downs with the prominent Firle Beacon in the far distance, across ripening summer fields. It was from near here that Rudyard Kipling was inspired to write of 'our blunt, bow headed, whale-backed Downs' with their 'bare slopes where chasing shadows skim'.

Blackdown. This view from Blackdown, the lofty sandstone ridge near to the north-western county border and the highest point in Sussex at 280m, looks south illustrating the degree of woodland still surviving within the area. Tennyson lived nearby at Aldworth House and from there wrote his famous lines:

You came, and looked and loved the view
Long-known and loved by me,
Green Sussex fading into blue
With one grey glimpse of sea.

Midhurst, Petworth
and
THE WESTERN HILL COUNTRY

The dramatic ruins of Cowdray House, just outside Midhurst, gutted by fire in 1793. Once a magnificent Tudor mansion built about 1520, the ivy-clad remains are now preserved including the almost intact kitchen that survived the fire.

Sandwiched between the northern chalk escarpment of the West Sussex Downs and the 'Low' Weald and extending from the Hampshire border eastwards to beyond the Arun valley is a region of hilly country developed on sandstone formations. This remarkably diverse 'secret' countryside with its many commons, heaths and woodlands has a distinctive character where the grey/buff stone has become a prominent building material. The two principal towns of Midhurst and Petworth situated here are linked by the western River Rother, at one time navigable from its junction with the River Arun to as far as Midhurst Quay.

The game of Polo has become synonymous with Cowdray Park, where it has been played since 1910. Polo is considered to be one of the oldest recorded games in the world. It has been a favourite pastime of royalty, most notably the Prince of Wales, who has frequently played at Cowdray. Gold Cup Day shown here is the highlight of the Cowdray season.

Midhurst grew up through the centuries to become an important market town and it is possible to trace its development through its attractive and traditional buildings, ranging from fifteenth-century timber framing to elegant Georgian brick and local stone. There was a castle here at one time but this was abandoned in the thirteenth century. The distinctive Cowdray yellow paintwork shown on the cottage (right) is a feature of the area.

The church of St George at Trotton is famous for its magnificent medieval brasses and wall paintings. It contains the earliest known brass of a woman, Margaret Camoys, seen here dating from 1310. Trotton's other famous brass is of Thomas, Lord Camoys, a hero of Agincourt and his wife Elizabeth, which dates from about 1419, one of the largest, most ornate and best preserved brasses in England.

The eleventh-century church of St Mary, Chithurst, stands on a knoll, possibly a pre-Christian site, above the banks of the River Rother. This tiny and simplest of churches has changed little over an entire millennium and Pevsner quotes 'that poverty or remoteness have kept the original dimensions intact without any kind of addition.' Some of the surrounding grave slabs are claimed to be nearly as old as the church itself. In this region there are many other examples of the simplest and most moving of churches dating from early periods and St Mary's, Bepton, St Andrew's, Didling (the shepherd's church) and St James's, Selham would be amongst them.

Hill country scenes. **Opposite:** Fittleworth Common consists of open woodland and being similar to many of the other commons in this hilly region is typical of Sussex Greensand heathland. Nearby Brinkwells was the home of Sir Edward Elgar between 1917 and 1921 where he wrote his Cello Concerto. **Above:** Autumn in Mens Wood. Mens Wood, bordering on to the Sussex Weald between Petworth and Wisborough Green, is regarded as one of the finest ancient woodlands in Europe and is a remaining fragment of the great Wealden Forest. Its name is derived from the Saxon word 'gemaennes' meaning a common.

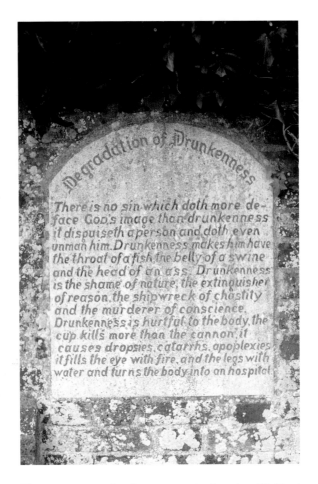

This warning to all pub-goers can be found at Kirdford
near Petworth.

The west front of Petworth House in its parkland setting was built during the last years of the seventeenth century as part of the great re-modelling of the house by the 6th Duke of Somerset who engaged master craftsmen such as the wood-carver Grinling Gibbons to work on the house's magnificent interior. The building incorporates the chapel (constructed in 1309) of the original fortified house that stood on the site. One of the glories of the house is its magnificent collection of paintings including works by Gainsborough, Rembrandt, Turner and Vandyke. During the 1750s Lancelot 'Capability' Brown landscaped the park, considered to be one of his greatest creations and the inspiration for some of Turner's paintings. By 1873 the house had passed to Lord Leconfield and by then the Petworth Estates encompassed some 12000 hectares of land.

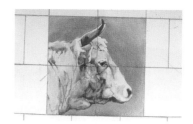

The town of Petworth has developed in the shadow of the great house and park and described by Cobbett in 1823 as 'a nice market town, but solid and clean'. Despite invasive traffic it is still a delight to walk around revealing a fascinating mix of styles and materials as shown by this selection of photographs.

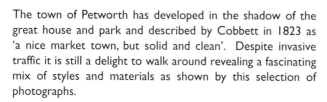

THE WESTERN HILL COUNTRY

Petworth Antique Market. Petworth has established itself today as one of Southern England's leading centres for antiques and with its numerous antique shops, house, park, museums and other attractions it has become a popular tourist destination.

The Monk's Common Room, Battle Abbey. The Abbey was founded by William the Conqueror as an act of thanksgiving for his victory in 1066 and as a mark of respect for those killed. It was built with the high altar of the church on the exact spot where King Harold died. Today little is left of the church, destroyed in the Dissolution, but the roofless Dormitory Block still stands and below it a series of undercroft rooms of which the Monk's Common Room, shown here, is one of the most moving. Here, with its vaulted stone ceiling coloured with age over the centuries, a certain spirit still survives of that October day when *the* battle of English history took place at this very location. Most of the remaining remodelled buildings of the site now form part of Battle Abbey School. Strictly speaking Battle is not a part of the Eastern Levels, being sited on the edge of the High Weald, but its history is closely linked.

Pevensey, Rye
and
THE EASTERN LEVELS

Roman walling, Pevensey Castle. A castle was built here in about 1100 shortly after the Norman invasion and within the walls of the third-century Roman fort of Anderida; a reminder of Pevensey's importance as a Cinque Port in medieval times long before the sea retreated over 2km to the south. Most of the Roman walls, described as the finest Roman monument in Sussex and enclosing an area of some 4ha, still stand and it was within these that William the Conqueror and his army spent their first night on English soil prior to the fateful battle.

Behind Pevensey almost flat, dyke-drained pasture land, the Pevensey Levels, stretch north towards the hillier Wealden country. Similarly around the now land-locked port of Rye, the Brede, East Guldeford, Pett and Rother Levels reach eastwards to merge with Romney Marsh as their rivers flow down from the Weald to the sea. This distinctive area, once highly vulnerable to French raids and with its history of a storm battered, retreating coastline and silting of ancient harbours, is sometimes known as the Eastern Levels.

Herstmonceaux Castle. The moated, brick Herstmonceaux Castle set in beautiful park-land was built around 1441 as a castellated manor house, one of the earliest important brick buildings in England. Becoming the home of the Dacre family for almost 300 years, it was eventually sold, part of the interior was demolished and by the late eighteenth century it was a ruin. Restoration was commenced in 1913 and finally completed some twenty years later. Towards the end of the 1940s it became the home of the Royal Greenwich Observatory and now with its modern Observatory Science Centre, it is a popular location to visit.

Morning reflections, Bodiam Castle. After the burning of Rye and Winchelsea by French marauders in the late fourteenth century and due to fears of a major French invasion up the estuary of the River Rother from the coast, the romantic Bodiam Castle was built as an additional means of defence of the adjacent countryside. Constructed as a perfect square with massive corner drum towers, the castle in its calm, wide moat has been described as 'the most fairy of English castles'. Never having to withstand attack from foreign invaders, the domestic interior was dismantled during the Civil War. Fortunately, however, after purchase in the nineteenth century, the then ruinous exterior was finally restored in 1919 by Lord Curzon and bequeathed to the National Trust.

Normans Bay. The low-lying coasts of East Sussex have always been an ideal landing area for any invading force. As a result a series of 46 circular brick fortifications known as Martello Towers were built between Eastbourne and Rye Harbour between 1805 and 1810 as a defence against a feared Napoleonic invasion. The towers, with walls up to 2m thick and with doors high above ground level, had a main gun mounted on the roof. They were sited at the back of beaches where landings seemed possible. Now, many have been demolished or washed away but ten still remain and this view of Normans Bay shows one of the towers with Eastbourne in the far distance. The name of Martello was derived from a structure that opposed British landings in Corsica during the late eighteenth century. A further tower was later built at Seaford and is now a museum.

The Royal Military Canal near Iden. This peaceful scene on the Rother Levels shows part of what was then the Sussex section of the Royal Military Canal. The canal, simply a wide dyke, was dug in 1804 as another response to suspicions of Napoleon. It ran around the north and west of Romney Marsh starting at Cliff End near Winchelsea in Sussex, reaching the Kent border near Iden, and then continued on to Shorncliffe in Kent itself. It would have acted as a buffer against the advance of any invading forces. Gun turrets were intended along its route but never built. A stone pillar on the edge of the canal marks the Sussex/Kent border near this location.

'The Truggery' workshop, Herstmonceaux. Herstmonceaux is generally regarded as the home of the trug making industry, a traditional craft in Sussex dating back over several hundred years. The word trug is possibly derived from the Anglo Saxon 'trog' meaning boat-shaped article. Trugs are baskets of local timber made in a similar fashion to clinker-built boats using age-old techniques such as sawing, shaving, soaking and steaming. The baskets are constructed in a variety of shapes and sizes using sweet chestnut and willow and were originally used for agricultural purposes but are now extremely popular with gardeners. Queen Victoria once ordered a consignment for her gardens.

Dacre Tomb, Herstmonceaux. The church of All Saints, Herstmonceaux, dating back generally to the thirteenth century houses the Dacre Chapel, one of the earliest examples of church brickwork in Sussex and added to the original building in about 1450. This small, beautiful chapel was given by the Fiennes family, then living in the nearby castle and contains the decorated Gothic monument erected in 1534 to the memory of Thomas, the 8th Lord Dacre and his son. Built of three varieties of stone, the monument is the chief ornament of the church. It features a table tomb with two carved and painted effigies of men in Milanese armour, each with hands in an attitude of prayer. Above them is a richly ornate canopy. During recent restoration work it has since been confirmed that the two figures are not of Lord Dacre and his son but of the half brothers Hooe, possibly brought from Battle Abbey after the Dissolution and altered to represent the Dacre family members.

Great Dixter. The fifteenth-century manor of Great Dixter near Northiam was purchased by Nathaniel Lloyd in 1910 and restored and extended under the guidance of the architect Edwin Lutyens, partly by the addition of a medieval hall house moved from Benenden in Kent. The surrounding gardens were also designed by Lutyens, the planting being carried out by Nathaniel and his wife. Cared for by the late Christopher Lloyd, the gardening writer, the gardens have in recent years become one of the most interesting, experimental and informal gardens in England. Wild meadows are used instead of lawns, there is the famous 'long border' of some 70m, a sunken garden with pool, extensive examples of decorative topiary and an exuberant exotic garden. Both house and the constantly changing gardens are open to the public, a popular venue for visitors from the continent and all gardening enthusiasts.

Rye Harbour. Rye Harbour is a separate community from the town of Rye itself and is situated out near the mouth of the River Rother on the marsh and shingle. Consisting of a scattering of sheds, old cottages, caravans and pubs, it has a distinctive character all of its own. Much of the surrounding land with its gravel pits and lagoons has now become part of the Rye Harbour Nature Reserve, a Site of Special Scientific Interest and regarded as one of the finest examples of shingle vegetation in Britain. The area is also used as a safe haven and stopover for many nesting and shore birds.

Church Square, Rye. The historic town of Rye, originally founded in the eleventh century, was built on a small island close to the sea, but as the sea receded, it has been left stranded almost 5km inland on a sandstone hill surrounded by flat fertile marshland. As one of the ancient Cinque Ports, it once had a busy harbour and despite frequent attacks by the French during the fourteenth and fifteenth centuries, the town retained much of its prosperity, recognised by the title of 'Rye Royal' bestowed upon it by Queen Elizabeth in 1573. As the sea began to retreat, the harbour slowly silted up to leave the town almost frozen in time clustered around its unique hilltop site with St Mary's Church at its apex. With its outstanding variety of closely-packed period buildings lining the often steep and narrow cobbled streets, the town's rich history is still very much in evidence and in the words of Arthur Mee 'is like no other town in England'. Today its once bustling quaysides echo to the sound of pleasure boats cruising along the River Rother and the footsteps of the many visitors from whom much of its income is now derived.

Aspects of Rye

Winchelsea. The original town of Winchelsea was destroyed by the sea's encroachment, particularly after the great storm of 1287. However, due to its strategic importance, a replacement new town was built on a raised promontory to the north of the old site. The then tidal estuary of the River Brede served the new town which under the direction of Edward I was laid out to a rigid grid of streets and occupied from 1288 onwards. Similarly to Rye, Winchelsea suffered from numerous French attacks but despite the planned ambitious scale of the town and its church of St Thomas, prosperity soon declined. The river became narrower as the sea retreated. From the end of the fifteenth century the partly-built town simply shrank back into the spacious, rather nostalgic and unusual village to be seen today approached from the harbour site through the remaining stone Strand and Pipewell Gates.

A view over the Rother Levels near Iden looking towards the Kent border and the Isle of Oxney. It is hard to believe that much of this land was at one time submerged by the sea providing access for ships using the numerous inland wharves and quays. These are now only accessible by small craft up narrow and shallow channels and the upper reaches of the various rivers.

Saxon detailing, Worth. The church of St Nicholas at Worth is considered to be one of the very finest Saxon churches remaining in Britain. Most of the structure has been dated as pre-eleventh century and many of its features such as the pilaster strips topped by a horizontal string course and the nave windows of two lights divided by a stumpy column are pure Saxon. Within the building the three great Saxon crossing arches are some of the largest to be found. Only the tower with its shingled spire has been added later. To enter the church from the bustle of nearby Crawley new town or the clamour of the adjacent M23 motorway is an enlightening experience when time can simply revert back over 1000 years. It is still not clearly understood why such a magnificent church was built in what was a part of the dense Wealden Forest.

East Grinstead, Horsham
and
THE SUSSEX WEALD

The backs of the pews at St George's Church, West Grinstead, with the names of local houses and farms whose owners had reserved seating for church services. The lettering dates back to the early nineteenth century and is a rare survival. The old Sussex names such as Buckells, Figland, Grinders, Hobshorts, North Fening, Patching, Pratts, Rookcross, Sunt and Whitefoots, are a reminder of the numerous farms once found in this area before many, along with the village itself, vanished.

The Sussex Weald spans the northern half of the county, a region once rich in ancient woodlands and coppice interrupted by areas of open heathland and small fields. To the north and east and extending into parts of Kent and Surrey is the hilly 'High' Weald mainly on sandstone formations reaching up to 240m at Crowborough Beacon and with its often distinctive deep, steep sided valleys. To the south stretching almost to the Downs lies the gently undulating, comparatively flat 'Low' Weald. Despite tremendous demands on land for new housing and industry, a distant view across the Weald still gives the impression of much unbroken woodland. The challenge of this forest barrier, the early difficult roads and wet, sticky, heavy clay soils of the 'Low' Weald made the Wealden region the least known area of Sussex for many centuries.

The Premonstratensian Bayham Abbey is undoubtedly the most impressive monastic ruin in Sussex. Quite literally straddling the Sussex/Kent border near Tunbridge Wells, the Abbey was built between 1208 and 1211 with gatehouses in both counties. In 1525 the monastery was suppressed and fell into a romantic ruin, which over the succeeding centuries, was used as a centrepiece to the landscaping of the immediate area by local landowners. Amongst these was Lord Camden who used the services of the designer Humphrey Repton on several occasions during the nineteenth century. The Abbey is now in the care of English Heritage.

Typical 'High' Weald hilly, wooded countryside near Brightling looking towards Burwash. It was this type of environment with its deep valleys, streams and brooks that prior to the art of road building left much of the Sussex Weald in a degree of physical and cultural isolation from the rest of the county and Southern England for so long. Even in the twenty-first century, it is still in part a region of secret places, silent waters and shadowy glades.

Hammer pond near Horsted Keynes. For centuries the 'High' Weald had been worked for iron, initially using simple bloomery processes, which changed drastically towards the end of the fifteenth century with the introduction of the blast furnace. The use of furnaces fuelled by abundant supplies of Wealden timber and with their bellows and forge hammers driven by waterpower from the dammed streams transformed many parts of the Weald. This in turn established the Sussex ironworks as the leading cast iron producers in the country during the first half of the sixteenth century. Iron was used to an increasing extent for arms, shipbuilding, domestic construction, firebacks etc and it was not until the more efficient development of the industry in other parts of the country that the Sussex furnaces and forges started to close, the last being at Ashburnham in the 1820s. The most distinctive remaining evidence of the iron industry today is the hammer pond. They were generally formed in a series along a dammed up stream, often in deep wooded valleys, to provide a more reliable flow to power the furnaces. The example shown here is one of a flight of ten such ponds at Horsted Keynes.

Details of three Sussex cast iron tomb slabs to be found in the church of St Peter and St Paul at Wadhurst. There are some 30 of these slabs within the church dating from 1617 – 1790 and indicate the importance of the iron industry in this area during the seventeenth and eighteeth centuries.

East Grinstead. Despite ever increasing traffic, East Grinstead's medieval past can still be traced by the layout of its High Street – an original broad street narrowed in part with an island of buildings which possibly replaced earlier market stalls. Each side of the street is lined with buildings, many of which date back to fourteenth – sixteenth century origins.

Left: Cromwell House from the early 1600s and reflecting the new found wealth from the Sussex iron industry.

Sackville College, an almshouse founded by Thomas Sackville, 2nd Earl of Dorset in 1619.

The timber-framed Priest House at West Hoathley not far from East Grinstead dates back to the early fifteenth century. It was probably built by the monks from Lewes Priory and like so many of the older, medieval Wealden houses it features a roof of Horsham flagged stone. These roofs were often constructed to a relatively steep pitch due to the immense weight imposed on the timber frame. The building was opened as a museum in 1908 and with its traditional cottage garden is now in the care of Sussex Past, the Sussex Archaeological Society.

Michelham Priory. The original Augustinian Priory was founded in 1229 but largely destroyed at the Dissolution, the remaining fragments being incorporated into a Tudor mansion. Situated on the banks of the River Cuckmere, the property is surrounded by the longest medieval water-filled moat in England and entered via the fourteenth-century stone gatehouse, part of which is shown here. Now, also cared for by Sussex Past, many of the buildings such as the watermill and Great Barn have been restored and together with the house and grounds are open to the public.

The Church of the Holy Sepulchre, Warminghurst. Another Wealden gem, this thirteenth-century remote church on a knoll north east of Storrington, with just a farmhouse for company, is now in the care of The Churches Conservation Trust. Its relatively plain exterior hides a remarkably unspoilt interior. Dividing the nave and chancel is a three-arch timber screen of about 1700 with a painting of the royal coat of arms of Queen Anne above, with surrounding drapery. Adjacent to the screen, the nave is filled with eighteenth-century pine box pews, a three-decker pulpit and clerk's desk with an enormous clerk's chair. The clear glass windows, uneven flagstone floor and memorials to the Butler and Shelley families complete this harmonious and memorable scene.

Bateman's, Burwash. The Jacobean house of Bateman's was built in 1634 by John Brittan, an ironmaster and is particularly well known as the home of Rudyard Kipling from 1902 until his death in 1936. Built of local sandstone, it is a fine example of the prosperity that the Sussex ironmasters enjoyed for a brief period, their houses often surpassing contemporary manor houses. Now owned by the National Trust, the building is kept as it was in Kipling's time.

Ashdown Forest. Ashdown Forest has been described by Peter Brandon (*The Sussex Landscape*) as 'the largest tract of wild scenery remaining in Sussex', an open region of high ground covered by isolated Scots pine, bracken, gorse and bell heather, broken only by enclosed areas of varying forms of wood and farmland. A decree of 1693 recognised commoners rights by preserving much of the forest as common grazing, awarding an area of some 2600ha for the purpose and therefore creating the foundations of the landscape to be seen today. The writer A. A. Milne who lived in Hartfield nearby used the forest as a setting for his characters of Winnie-the-Pooh and friends and a memorial to Milne and his illustrator E. H. Shepard is sited at Gill's Lap near this photograph. William Cobbett's view was somewhat different 'a heath with here and there a few birch shrubs upon it, verily the most villainously ugly spot I ever saw in England!'

High Rocks, near Tunbridge Wells. The 'High' Wealden sandstone formations often end dramatically in a series of cliffs with the rocks eroded and weathered to smooth, sometimes rounded and buttressed profiles over thousands of years. High Rocks, literally a few metres within the Sussex/Kent border near Tunbridge Wells is a fine example. Here the rock faces rise to a height of up to 25 metres and became a popular place to visit from Victorian times. Once used as shelter by Wealden hunting parties and later as a hill fort, evidence has been found of human occupation dating back to at least 4000BC. Similar evidence has also been found at Hermitage Rocks, High Hurstwood and other greensand areas of the Weald. Note the carved graffiti of the 1830s.

The coming of the railways transformed Sussex as elsewhere and the 37-arched 450m long Balcombe Viaduct spanning the Ouse valley is one of England's most impressive railway structures. Carrying the London-Brighton main line, the viaduct was designed by John Rastrick and completed for the first trains that ran on 21 September 1841. It is hard to believe that many of the 12 million bricks and much of the stone used in its construction were carried by barge up what now appears to be a very small tributary of the Ouse below the viaduct. It is also unusual to find that each pier is arched at the bottom as well as the top as shown here from below the massive structure. It was the opening of the railways that enabled many of the coastal resorts to become popular destinations for short holidays. Day trippers began to arrive and the pattern of commuting to London also started – a trend that continues to this day.

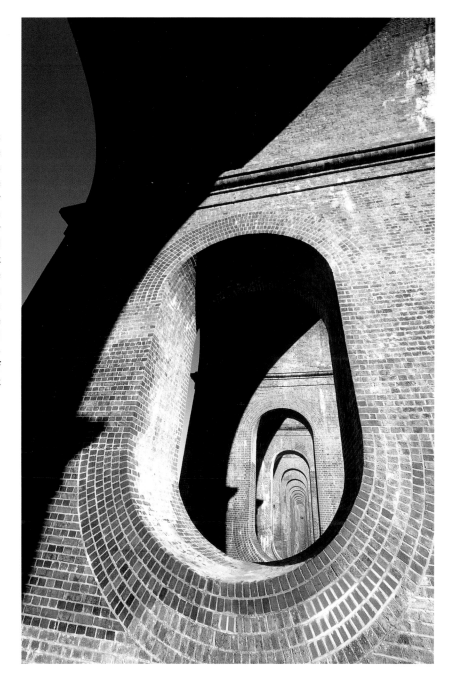

This page and opposite: The Bluebell Railway was founded by a group of dedicated enthusiasts, in conjunction with local inhabitants, with the aim of re-opening a part of the old Lewes-East Grinstead branch line finally closed by British Railways in 1958. Initially the line was re-opened between Sheffield Park and Horsted Keynes stations in 1960, later reaching Kingscote and with work now well under way for a final return back to East Grinstead. As such the railway has become a world famous steam preservation centre and is the only all-steam standard gauge preserved railway in the country. It is still run throughout the year by enthusiastic volunteers supported by a small group of full-time staff and over the last forty-five or so years has carried millions of passengers. These two pages illustrate a few aspects of this remarkable undertaking. Other preserved 'heritage' railways in Sussex include part of the Kent and East Sussex Railway between Bodiam and Tenterden, the Spa Valley Railway from Tunbridge Wells and the Lavender Line based at Isfield.

Sheffield Park Gardens. From the late eighteenth century onwards, the appearance of the Weald started to change through the effects of landscaping. High Wealden heaths were planted with clumps of Scots pine and the commons with conifers, the heavy, often acidic clays being particularly suited to the growth of trees and shrubs. Many of the wealthy landed gentry started to create magnificent gardens around their country homes and those at Sheffield Park, laid out by 'Capability' Brown for the first Earl of Sheffield, were some of the earliest. Transformed at the start of the twentieth century, the 50ha gardens are amongst the finest of their type in the country with many exotic species in a lakeside setting overlooked by the house itself, designed in 1775. The internationally renowned gardens are now in the care of the National Trust and are particularly colourful during the autumn season.

Wakehurst Place. The ornamental gardens in the hilly environment of Wakehurst Place were created by Gerald Loder from 1903 onwards around the much-altered mansion dating back to 1590. Containing one of the world's finest collection of plants, many exotic and rare trees and flowering shrubs are featured in areas including a Himalayan glade, water garden, a winter garden, Asian heath, wetlands and extensive wood-lands. Bequeathed to the National Trust, the gardens are now leased to the Royal Botanic Gardens at Kew and in particular include the newly constructed Millennium Seed Bank. Gerald Loder was the younger brother of Sir Edmund Loder who created another of the glorious Wealden gardens at Leonardslee.

Standen House near East Grinstead was built in the early 1890s as a country retreat for James Beale and is regarded as one of the finest designs of the architect Philip Webb. With its exterior using many traditional and local building materials, the house's richly furnished interior features original textiles and wallpaper designed by William Morris and pottery by William de Morgan. Often described as a showpiece of the Arts and Crafts movement, the house is surrounded by beautiful informal hillside gardens and woodland and again is in the care of the National Trust.

Nymans Gardens at Handcross, not far from Crawley, contain the partly burnt-out romantic shell of a pseudo-medieval manor built in the 1920s and destroyed by fire in 1947. The extensive gardens were begun by Ludwig Messel in the 1890s and continued by successive generations of the family with the ruin later acting as a fine centrepiece. There are many rare plants, shrubs and trees and with the gardens being situated on high ground, extensive views can be obtained towards the distant South Downs. Bequeathed to the National Trust in 1954, many of the trees were sadly destroyed in the Great Storm of 1987 but now much replanting has taken place. Other notable gardens in Sussex include Borde Hill near Haywards Heath, Denmans at Fontwell, High Beeches also near Handcross, Highdown behind Worthing, Parham near Storrington and Pashley Manor at Ticehurst.

Queen's Square, Crawley. Despite the 'new town' suffix, Crawley was once a small medieval town and the wide High Street with buildings dating back to the fifteenth century acts as a reminder of this period. Becoming an early post-war 'new town' in 1947, it grew rapidly, spreading out across the countryside and up to neighbouring Gatwick to create one of the largest urban areas in Sussex. With Gatwick Airport now designated as London's second airport, development still continues. The new town's shopping centre, built immediately adjacent to the old High Street, is typical of the 1950s – 1960s era but the decorative iron bandstand within Queen's Square (in the background of the photograph) is an interesting feature. This was originally constructed in 1891 at the old Gatwick racecourse but sold to Crawley Development Corporation and re-erected in the square when Queen Elizabeth II opened both the square and the new Gatwick Airport in 1958.

The Causeway, Horsham. In a similar manner to Crawley and East Grinstead, Horsham's past has almost become hidden by modern development and twenty-first-century traffic. However, The Causeway marks one end of what used to be a large, tapering, wedge-shaped green dating back to the medieval period. Becoming an important borough and market town, buildings slowly spread around this green and across its centre leaving both ends relatively open to form The Carfax to the north and The Causeway to the south. Leading down to the thirteenth-century Parish Church of St Mary, The Causeway has now become a delightful tree-lined oasis with a succession of period town houses in a variety of local materials and styles along its sides. It is a welcome contrast to many of the town's busier aspects.

This page and opposite: The South of England Show, Ardingly. Ardingly is home to the South of England Showground where the show itself is held each year and where numerous other rallies, fairs, exhibitions and large-scale events are also staged. The show provides a popular mix of entertainment over several days including numerous sales, trade and catering outlets and stands; crafts, flower and horticultural displays; exhibitions, local society features, farming and livestock demonstrations and all other matters of an agricultural nature. There are events held throughout each day in the many arenas and marquees and the entire show becomes an occasion to bring out the sunshine in every sense of the word.

Cricket at Chichester. The Prebendal School playing cricket on Westgate Fields in Chichester with the City Walls and Cathedral beyond. The once famous view of the Cathedral seen across rural fields from the bypass has slowly been eroded by modern development, an inner ring road and the formation of the school sports facilities. However, despite these changes, much of the charm and excitement of the scene remains as shown here. The Prebendal School is the oldest in Sussex, its origins going back to the time when the Cathedral was begun in the late eleventh century.

A SUSSEX MISCELLANY

Cricket bat manufacture, Robertsbridge. The village of Robertsbridge is particularly well known as the home of the Gray-Nicholls cricket bat factory. Founded by L. J. Nicholls, the village carpenter and an enthusiastic cricketer who first started to make bats for friends in the 1870s, the company soon established an international reputation. Merging with the sports equipment manufacturer H. J. Gray and Sons in 1940, Gray-Nicholls have gone from strength to strength and their bats, still made at Robertsbridge, are acknowledged as some of the best in the market. The hand-made bats of English willow and cane require some seventy different stages in manufacture and have been used by nearly all the famous test cricketers worldwide.

Racing at Goodwood was begun by the 3rd Duke of Richmond in 1801 and with the erection of a grandstand in 1830 and subsequent nineteenth-century improvements, the meetings soon became an important event in the social calendar. It was King George VI's sentiment that racing at Goodwood 'is a garden party with racing tacked on' that has been endorsed over the years by race goers and which has created the unique Goodwood atmosphere still to be found today. Situated high up with magnificent views over the Downs, the course has constantly been updated with new stands and facilities and with the introduction of evening and Sunday racing is as popular as ever. 'Glorious Goodwood' week during July is still regarded by many as the place to be and to be seen and a notable feature of the English summer season. The Goodwood motor circuit meetings nearby, revived in 1998, together with the Goodwood Festival of Speed, initiated in 1993, both under the inspiration of Charles March, grandson of the 9th Duke of Richmond, have also become phenomenally successful events attracting stars and cars from all over the world.

The annual London to Brighton cycle ride was first held in 1975 and the photograph shows riders completing the 2005 event along Madeira Drive adjacent to Brighton's seafront. Starting at half hourly intervals, the ride attracted over 27,000 cyclists on this particular occasion, all cycling in aid of the event's main charity the British Heart Foundation which hoped to make some £3m from the day. The fast, enthusiastic riders are given early departure times enabling them to reach the resort for breakfast whilst the vast majority of entrants arrive in Brighton throughout the remainder of the day making it literally, and particularly for their legs, an outing to remember! Other notable annual London to Brighton events include the famous Veteran car run dating back to 1896, the Pioneer motor cycle run, first started in 1937 and the Commercial Vehicle run.

'Harmer' plaques. In several East Sussex churchyards, headstones can be found with delicately designed terra cotta tablets or plaques inset into the stone. These were produced by Jonathan Harmer, son of a Heathfield stonemason, from the late eighteenth century until his death in 1849. The tablets vary in colour from a buff to bright red and are found in a variety of different designs, of which the basket of fruit and flowers, shown here, is probably the most common. This example is located in Salehurst churchyard near Robertsbridge.

Lest we forget. Frescoes, Victory Hall, Balcombe. The Victory Hall at the small mid-Sussex village of Balcombe was built in 1923 as a memorial to Balcombe men who had fought and died in the First World War. It was funded by public subscription and by the generosity of Lady Denman. Around the upper walls of the hall are a series of frescoes painted by Neville Lytton based on his experiences of the horrors of trench warfare and as a war correspondent in France. Using a 'true fresco' technique, the paint was applied to the wet plaster giving the images a durability and monumental appearance. On the north 'peace wall' are portraits of known people, some from the village, including the artist and Lady Denman. On the south and east walls, the pain, misery, hate and despair of war are depicted – part of which is shown here. The figures of Dolor and Spes (Sorrow and Hope) appear on the west wall. Neville Lytton wished to convey his hopes for reconciliation and peace and a trust in the future for the people of Balcombe.

Church paintings. Wall paintings, murals and frescoes have been used within churches for many centuries as a means of communication and teaching. The painted ceiling of the English Martyrs Church at Goring, near Worthing, is however totally unique. Carried out solely by Gary Evans over a five-and-a-half-year period, with full support from the church authorities and completed in 1993, it is an exact copy of the restored ceiling in the Sistine Chapel in Rome painted by Michaelangelo. The colours were made to match the original and the final artwork has been reduced to about two-thirds scale. The ceiling at Goring is an amazing example of one person's religious inspiration and is the only known reproduction of the Sistine Chapel ceiling in the world.

Some of the finest surviving Norman church paintings remain in the simplest of buildings and these three examples of twelfth century paintings from the Lewes Cluniac School are among the best in Sussex. Being too poor, the churches were never 'restored' or 'improved' to any great extent and often the paintings were simply whitewashed over rather than being destroyed. Rediscovered from the nineteenth century onwards, the sometimes rich, sometimes faded scenes are now treasured survivors of Norman art.

Right: The undedicated church at Coombes overlooking the Adur valley.

Left: St John's at Clayton below the Downs and **above:** St Botolph's at Hardham near Pulborough.

The Sussex countryside is particularly rich in its use of different local building materials. These can range from sea-rounded cobblestones and 'Mixon' stone of the coastal plain to the flint and chalk clunch of the Downland villages or the buff, grey or green coloured stone of the lower greensand region around Midhurst and Petworth. They can be the varying 'reds' of the 'Low' Wealden bricks and tile hanging, the painted weatherboarding in the vicinity of the Eastern Levels or the warm coloured sandstone of the 'High' Weald.

Timber was however the most commonly used of all materials until the general 'rebuilding' during the sixteenth and seventeenth centuries when chimneys were inserted, windows glazed and extensions added. Often the timber frame was retained but more durable materials used in conjunction. These two pages of Sussex village scenes and cottages illustrate a few of these aspects.

A late winter's afternoon at Chanctonbury Ring. This Iron Age hillfort, planted with beech trees in 1760 by Charles Goring, became one of the best known and most distinctive summits of the South Downs. Decimated by the Storm of 1987, the ring has now been replanted and it is hoped that one day it will again be looked upon as one of the great sights of Sussex. Cissbury Ring 4km to the south, behind Worthing, is one of the largest hillforts in Southern England. Within its circumference are the remains of a series of Neolithic flint mines dating back over 4000 years.

Sunset over Pagham Harbour. Pagham Harbour is one of the few undeveloped areas of the coast in West Sussex. The open landscape still retains a sense of wilderness and is popular with ornithologists. Reclaimed for agriculture in the late nineteenth century, the harbour was flooded again by storm in the early twentieth century. The harbour and surrounding pastures are now of international importance for wintering wildfowl and wading birds and much of it is managed as a local nature reserve. The chapel at nearby Church Norton is all that remains of Selsey's former parish church, which was removed to its present site in Selsey in 1866. It has been speculated that the original church may have been built near to the site of St Wilfred's Cathedral Church, now lost to the sea.

ACKNOWLEDGEMENTS

I would like to thank the many people who have helped me in the compilation of this book by allowing photography, providing information and for advising on or contributing to captions and text. I am therefore most grateful to the following:

Pam Malins and the Balcombe Victory Hall Management Committee; Keith Masters (Chichester Cathedral); Richard Pailthorpe; Sarah Philip (Charleston Trust); Charles Upton; Peter Zwinkels (Madestein UK); The management and staff at The Bluebell Railway, The Churches Conservation Trust, English Heritage, English Martyrs Church–Goring, Fishbourne Roman Palace, Great Dixter Charitable Trust, Grey-Nicholls, Herstmonceux Castle, The High Rocks, Lancing College Chapel, The National Trust, Petworth Antique Market, The Royal Botanic Gardens Kew, Sussex Past – The Sussex Archaeological Society and The Truggery, Herstmonceux.

In particular I wish to thank Joy for her infinite patience, support and hard work in typing the manuscript and of course Steven Pugsley and his colleagues at Halsgrove for their assistance throughout the project.

Finally, thoughts of my late Father who did his best to instill within me his own loving feelings towards Sussex, a county that I have treasured from an early age.

REFERENCE SOURCES

There are numerous books, booklets, papers, leaflets and guides about the county of Sussex. It is an impossible task to mention them all but the following have been invaluable as reference sources:

Arscott, D *Curiosities of West Sussex* SB Publications, 1993

Arscott, D *In Praise of Sussex* Pomegranate, 1996

Arscott, D *Dead and Buried in Sussex* S B Publications, 1997

Brabbs, D *Abbeys and Monasteries* Weidenfeld & Nicolson, 1999

Brandon, P *The Sussex Landscape* Hodder & Stoughton, 1974

Brandon, P *The South Downs* Phillimore, 1998

George, M *The South Downs* Pavilion, 1992

Hamilton Ellis, C *The London Brighton and South Coast Railway* Ian Allan, 1960

Hole, J and McGowan, I *Mundham & Runcton* MMM & BC, 2000

Jenkins, S *England's Thousand Best Churches* Penguin Books, 1999

Larkin, P *High Windows* Faber & Faber, 1974

Lesley, K and Short, B *An Historical Atlas of Sussex* Phillimore 1999

Lloyd, D *Historic Towns of Kent and Sussex* Victor Gollancz, 1991

McGowan, I *A Portrait of Brighton & Hove* Halsgrove, 2004

Mee, A *The Kings England: Sussex* Hodder & Stoughton, 1964

Mitchell, W *East Sussex – A Shell guide* Faber & Faber, 1978

Mitchell, R and Vann, J *Sussex – A Kipling Anthology* Padda Books, 1990

Nairn, I and Pevsner, N *The Buildings of England: Sussex* Penguin Books, 1975

Pailthorpe, R and McGowan, I *Chichester A Contemporary View* John Wiley, 1994

Pailthorpe, R and McGowan, I *Chichester A Millennium View* John Wiley, 2000

Sellman, D and Arscott, D *Sussex A Colour Portrait* Countryside Books, 2004

Skinner, D *Sussex – People and History* Crowood Press, 2002

Smith, B and Haas, P *Writers in Sussex* Radcliffe, 1985

Swinfen, W and Arscott, D *Hidden Sussex* BBC Radio Sussex, 1984

Talbot, R and Whiteman, R *The Garden of England* Weidenfeld & Nicolson, 1995

Tellem, G *Brighton and Sussex* Jarrold, 2001

Wales, T *A Sussex Garland* Godfrey Cave Associates, 1979

Guides and leaflets to the many attractions, museums, places of interest and churches featured within this book.